Frogs

Steve Parish

ANIMALS are Fun!

For a free color catalog describing Gareth Stevens Publishing's list of high-quality books and multimedia programs, call 1-800-542-2595 (USA) or 1-800-461-9120 (Canada). Gareth Stevens Publishing's Fax: (414) 225-0377.

Library of Congress Cataloging-in-Publication Data available upon request from the publisher. Fax: (414) 225-0377 for the attention of the Publishing Records Department.

ISBN 0-8368-2613-2

First published in North America in 2000 by
Gareth Stevens Publishing
1555 North RiverCenter Drive, Suite 201
Milwaukee, WI 53212 USA

This edition © 2000 by Gareth Stevens, Inc.
Additional end matter © 2000 by Gareth Stevens, Inc.

First published in 1998 by Steve Parish Publishing Pty. Ltd., P. O. Box 1058, Archerfield, BC, Queensland 4108, Australia. Original edition © 1998 by Steve Parish Publishing Pty. Ltd. Photography and creative direction by Steve Parish with special thanks to Hans and Judy Beste (front cover, title page, pp. 2, 6, 11), Darran Leal (p. 5), Ian Morris (pp. 8, 12, 13, 16), and Stan Breeden (small insets: title page, pp. 3, 6, 8, 11, 13, 15). Text by F. Melanie Lever, Kate Lovett, and Pat Slater, SPP.

U.S. author: Amy Bauman

Printed in the United States of America

1 2 3 4 5 6 7 8 9 04 03 02 01 00

Gareth Stevens Publishing
MILWAUKEE

Frogs belong to a group of animals called amphibians.

They begin life in the water but can later live on land.

A frog lays a mass of eggs.
The eggs hatch into tadpoles.

The tadpoles slowly grow and develop into frogs.

In order to breathe, a frog must keep its body cool and moist.

For this reason, frogs live in wet places. They are active at night.

Some types of
frogs live in water.

Other frogs live in trees. They have special toes for climbing.

When the weather is dry, some frogs live in holes in the ground.

A frog feeds on insects and other small animals, even other frogs!

Certain frogs have markings that show they are poisonous.

The tiny Javelin frog is only ½ inch (1½ centimeters) long.

The large cane toad grows to 9½ inches (24 cm) long.

Scientists are studying why many types of frogs have vanished.

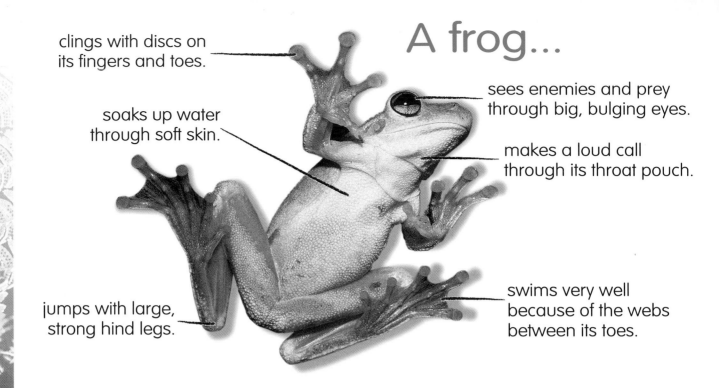

A frog...

clings with discs on its fingers and toes.

soaks up water through soft skin.

jumps with large, strong hind legs.

sees enemies and prey through big, bulging eyes.

makes a loud call through its throat pouch.

swims very well because of the webs between its toes.

Glossary/Index

amphibians — members of a group of cold-blooded animals, such as frogs, toads, and newts, that have gilled young. Gills are organs that obtain oxygen from water 2, 3

centimeter (cm) — in the metric system, a measurement equal to 0.394 inch 13, 14

markings — in the natural world, the pattern of color that sets one type of animal apart from another. Stripes and spots are examples of markings 12

mass — a large amount 4

moist — slightly wet; damp 6

poisonous — filled with toxins 12

scientists — people who have gained knowledge about general truths and general laws 15

tadpoles — young toads or frogs. Tadpoles have round bodies with long tails, fins, and gills 4, 5

vanished — disappeared 15